This Book

Belongs to

____

PREFACE

Use this in teaching your children about the "Power of Yet".

This activity follows the growth mindset teaching, There are three spaces for them to write things they already know how to do, one space to write something they don't YET know how to do, and additional page to reflect on how they can learn.

Allow your child to make time for what's important and spend the time filling out the reflection page, They will learn to appreciate and enjoy the little things while working towards their goals.

It's the little moments that brighten our days and bring joy, Be in the moment as much as we can, be mindful of our emotions and experiences, and always make time for fun and play.

And this easy to use journal is sure to help kids tap into that extraordinary power for the first time, Through writing and drawing, children will learn to give daily thanks for the good in their lives.

CONTENTS

HOW TO

1) BRAINSTORMING WITH YOUR KIDS

HAVE A CONVERSATION WITH YOUR CHILD ABOUT THE ACTIVITY IDEAS THAT YOU CAN DO WITH YOUR CHILDREN AND TALKING ABOUT THE "POWER OF YET."
(100 FUN IDEAS - PAGE 127)

2) PRACTICE A GROWTH MINDSET

THERE ARE THREE SPACES FOR THEM TO WRITE THINGS THEY ALREADY KNOW HOW TO DO, ONE SPACE TO WRITE SOMETHING THEY DON'T YET KNOW HOW TO DO, AND ADDITIONAL PAGE TO REFLECT ON HOW THEY CAN LEARN.

3) ACHIEVE THE GOAL

ONCE EACH LEARNING IS COMPLETED, WRITE YOUR MEMORIES AND IMPRESSIONS DOWN ON THE BOOK. BE SURE TO INCLUDE YOUR CHILDREN THOUGHTS, TOO!

GROWTH MINDSET THE POWER OF YET ACTIVITY

DATE:

S   M   T   W   TH   F   S   __ / __ / __

I CAN DO MANY THING.

1) I CAN:

2) I CAN:

3) I CAN:

SOME TING THAT I CANT'T DO YET, BUT I WILL KEEP TRYING LEARNING UNTIL I CAN.

I CAN'T DO....

....

....

....

WAYS I CAN GET THERE....

....

....

....

BECAUSE I....

....

....

....

DRAW A PICTURE TO SHOW HOW YOU USE YOUR BEAUTIFUL BRAIN TO SOLVE A PROBLEM.

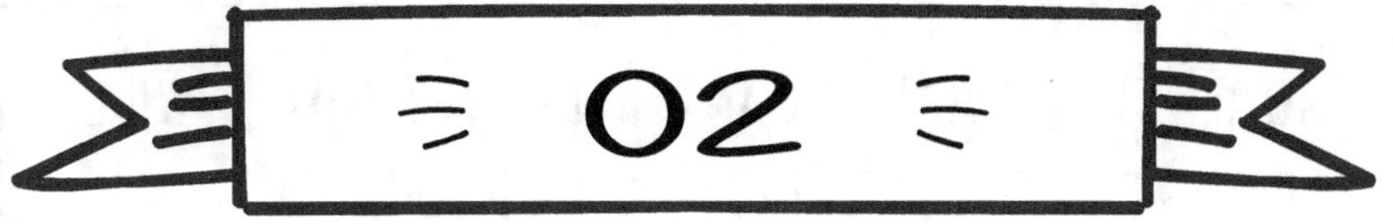

GROWTH MINDSET THE POWER OF YET ACTIVITY

DATE:

S   M   T   W   TH   F   S   __/__/__

I CAN DO MANY THING.

....

1) I CAN:
....

....

....

2) I CAN:
....

....

....

3) I CAN:
....

....

....

SOME TING THAT I CANT'T DO YET, BUT I WILL KEEP TRYING LEARNING UNTIL I CAN.

I CAN'T DO....

WAYS I CAN GET THERE....

BECAUSE I....

DRAW A PICTURE TO SHOW HOW YOU USE YOUR BEAUTIFUL BRAIN TO SOLVE A PROBLEM.

GROWTH MINDSET THE POWER OF YET ACTIVITY

DATE:

S   M   T   W   TH   F   S   __/__/__

I CAN DO MANY THING.

....

1) I CAN:

....

....

2) I CAN:

....

....

3) I CAN:

....

....

SOME TING THAT I CANT'T DO YET, BUT I WILL
KEEP TRYING LEARNING UNTIL I CAN.

I CAN'T DO....

....

....

....

WAYS I CAN GET THERE....

....

....

....

BECAUSE I....

....

....

....

DRAW A PICTURE TO SHOW HOW YOU USE YOUR BEAUTIFUL BRAIN TO SOLVE A PROBLEM.

GROWTH MINDSET THE POWER OF YET ACTIVITY

DATE:

S   M   T   W   TH   F   S   __/__/__

I CAN DO MANY THING.

....

1) I CAN:
....

....

....

2) I CAN:
....

....

....

3) I CAN:
....

....

SOME TING THAT I CANT'T DO YET, BUT I WILL KEEP TRYING LEARNING UNTIL I CAN.

I CAN'T DO....

....

....

....

WAYS I CAN GET THERE....

....

....

....

BECAUSE I....

....

....

....

DRAW A PICTURE TO SHOW HOW YOU USE YOUR BEAUTIFUL BRAIN TO SOLVE A PROBLEM.

GROWTH MINDSET THE POWER OF YET ACTIVITY

DATE:

S   M   T   W   TH   F   S   __ / __ / __

I CAN DO MANY THING.

1) I CAN:

2) I CAN:

3) I CAN:

SOME TING THAT I CANT'T DO YET, BUT I WILL KEEP TRYING LEARNING UNTIL I CAN.

I CAN'T DO....

....

....

....

WAYS I CAN GET THERE....

....

....

....

BECAUSE I....

....

....

....

DRAW A PICTURE TO SHOW HOW YOU USE YOUR BEAUTIFUL BRAIN TO SOLVE A PROBLEM.

GROWTH MINDSET THE POWER OF YET ACTIVITY

DATE:

S M T W TH F S ___/___/___

I CAN DO MANY THING.

....

1) I CAN:

....

....

2) I CAN:

....

....

3) I CAN:

....

....

SOME TING THAT I CANT'T DO YET, BUT I WILL KEEP TRYING LEARNING UNTIL I CAN.

I CAN'T DO....

....

....

....

WAYS I CAN GET THERE....

....

....

....

BECAUSE I....

....

....

....

DRAW A PICTURE TO SHOW HOW YOU USE YOUR BEAUTIFUL BRAIN TO SOLVE A PROBLEM.

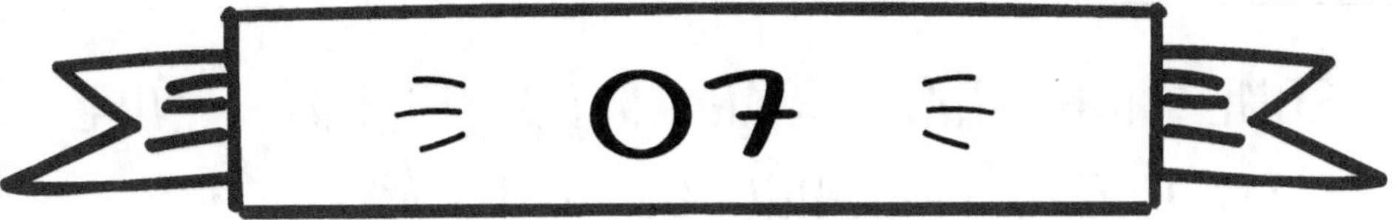

GROWTH MINDSET THE POWER OF YET ACTIVITY

DATE:

S   M   T   W   TH   F   S   __/__/__

I CAN DO MANY THING.

....

1) I CAN:

....

....

....

2) I CAN:

....

....

....

3) I CAN:

....

....

....

SOME TING THAT I CANT'T DO YET, BUT I WILL KEEP TRYING LEARNING UNTIL I CAN.

I CAN'T DO....

WAYS I CAN GET THERE....

BECAUSE I....

DRAW A PICTURE TO SHOW HOW YOU USE YOUR BEAUTIFUL BRAIN TO SOLVE A PROBLEM.

GROWTH MINDSET THE POWER OF YET ACTIVITY

DATE:

S   M   T   W   TH   F   S   __/__/__

I CAN DO MANY THING.

1) I CAN:

2) I CAN:

3) I CAN:

SOME TING THAT I CANT'T DO YET, BUT I WILL KEEP TRYING LEARNING UNTIL I CAN.

I CAN'T DO....

....

....

....

WAYS I CAN GET THERE....

....

....

....

BECAUSE I....

....

....

....

DRAW A PICTURE TO SHOW HOW YOU USE YOUR BEAUTIFUL BRAIN TO SOLVE A PROBLEM.

GROWTH MINDSET THE POWER OF YET ACTIVITY

DATE:

S   M   T   W   TH   F   S   __/__/__

I CAN DO MANY THING.

1) I CAN:

2) I CAN:

3) I CAN:

SOME TING THAT I CANT'T DO YET, BUT I WILL KEEP TRYING LEARNING UNTIL I CAN.

I CAN'T DO....

....

....

....

WAYS I CAN GET THERE....

....

....

....

BECAUSE I....

....

....

....

DRAW A PICTURE TO SHOW HOW YOU USE YOUR BEAUTIFUL BRAIN TO SOLVE A PROBLEM.

GROWTH MINDSET THE POWER OF YET ACTIVITY

DATE:

S   M   T   W   TH   F   S   __ / __ / __

I CAN DO MANY THING.

1) I CAN:

2) I CAN:

3) I CAN:

SOME TING THAT I CANT'T DO YET, BUT I WILL KEEP TRYING LEARNING UNTIL I CAN.

I CAN'T DO....

....

....

....

WAYS I CAN GET THERE....

....

....

....

BECAUSE I....

....

....

....

DRAW A PICTURE TO SHOW HOW YOU USE YOUR BEAUTIFUL BRAIN TO SOLVE A PROBLEM.

GROWTH MINDSET THE POWER OF YET ACTIVITY

DATE:

S   M   T   W   TH   F   S   ___/___/___

I CAN DO MANY THING.

1) I CAN:

2) I CAN:

3) I CAN:

SOME TING THAT I CANT'T DO YET, BUT I WILL KEEP TRYING LEARNING UNTIL I CAN.

I CAN'T DO....

....

....

....

WAYS I CAN GET THERE....

....

....

....

BECAUSE I....

....

....

....

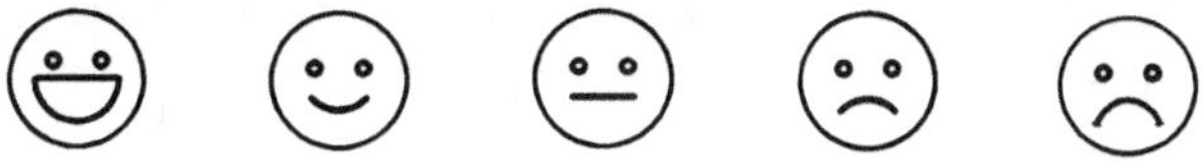

DRAW A PICTURE TO SHOW HOW YOU USE YOUR BEAUTIFUL BRAIN TO SOLVE A PROBLEM.

GROWTH MINDSET THE POWER OF YET ACTIVITY

DATE:

S M T W TH F S   __ / __ / __

I CAN DO MANY THING.

1) I CAN:

2) I CAN:

3) I CAN:

SOME TING THAT I CANT'T DO YET, BUT I WILL KEEP TRYING LEARNING UNTIL I CAN.

I CAN'T DO....

....

....

....

WAYS I CAN GET THERE....

....

....

....

BECAUSE I....

....

....

....

DRAW A PICTURE TO SHOW HOW YOU USE YOUR BEAUTIFUL BRAIN TO SOLVE A PROBLEM.

GROWTH MINDSET THE POWER OF YET ACTIVITY

DATE:

S   M   T   W   TH   F   S   __/__/__

I CAN DO MANY THING.

1) I CAN:

2) I CAN:

3) I CAN:

SOME TING THAT I CANT'T DO YET, BUT I WILL KEEP TRYING LEARNING UNTIL I CAN.

I CAN'T DO....

WAYS I CAN GET THERE....

BECAUSE I....

DRAW A PICTURE TO SHOW HOW YOU USE YOUR BEAUTIFUL BRAIN TO SOLVE A PROBLEM.

GROWTH MINDSET THE POWER OF YET ACTIVITY

DATE:

S   M   T   W   TH   F   S   ___/___/___

I CAN DO MANY THING.

1) I CAN:

2) I CAN:

3) I CAN:

SOME TING THAT I CANT'T DO YET, BUT I WILL KEEP TRYING LEARNING UNTIL I CAN.

I CAN'T DO....

....

....

....

WAYS I CAN GET THERE....

....

....

....

BECAUSE I....

....

....

....

DRAW A PICTURE TO SHOW HOW YOU USE YOUR BEAUTIFUL BRAIN TO SOLVE A PROBLEM.

GROWTH MINDSET THE POWER OF YET ACTIVITY

DATE:

S   M   T   W   TH   F   S   ___/___/___

I CAN DO MANY THING.

1) I CAN:

2) I CAN:

3) I CAN:

SOME TING THAT I CANT'T DO YET, BUT I WILL KEEP TRYING LEARNING UNTIL I CAN.

I CAN'T DO....

....

....

....

WAYS I CAN GET THERE....

....

....

....

BECAUSE I....

....

....

....

DRAW A PICTURE TO SHOW HOW YOU USE YOUR BEAUTIFUL BRAIN TO SOLVE A PROBLEM.

GROWTH MINDSET THE POWER OF YET ACTIVITY

DATE:

S M T W TH F S   __/__/__

I CAN DO MANY THING.

....

1) I CAN:

....

....

....

2) I CAN:

....

....

....

3) I CAN:

....

....

....

SOME TING THAT I CANT'T DO YET, BUT I WILL KEEP TRYING LEARNING UNTIL I CAN.

I CAN'T DO....

WAYS I CAN GET THERE....

BECAUSE I....

DRAW A PICTURE TO SHOW HOW YOU USE YOUR BEAUTIFUL BRAIN TO SOLVE A PROBLEM.

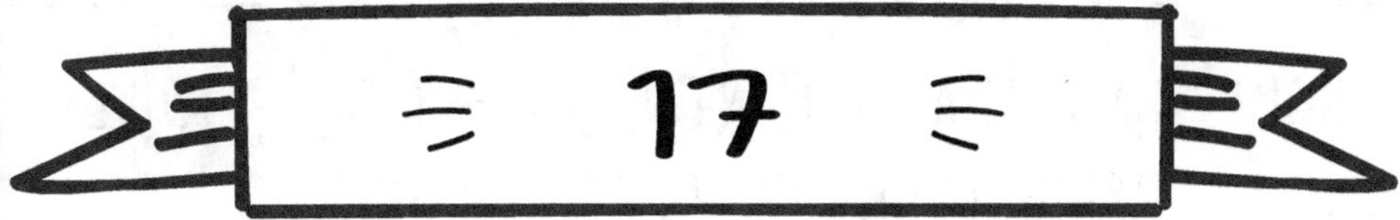

GROWTH MINDSET THE POWER OF YET ACTIVITY

DATE:

S   M   T   W   TH   F   S   __/__/__

I CAN DO MANY THING.

....

1) I CAN:

....

....

....

2) I CAN:

....

....

....

3) I CAN:

....

....

....

SOME TING THAT I CANT'T DO YET, BUT I WILL KEEP TRYING LEARNING UNTIL I CAN.

I CAN'T DO....

WAYS I CAN GET THERE....

BECAUSE I....

DRAW A PICTURE TO SHOW HOW YOU USE YOUR BEAUTIFUL BRAIN TO SOLVE A PROBLEM.

GROWTH MINDSET THE POWER OF YET ACTIVITY

DATE:

S   M   T   W   TH   F   S   ___/___/___

I CAN DO MANY THING.

1) I CAN:

2) I CAN:

3) I CAN:

SOME TING THAT I CANT'T DO YET, BUT I WILL KEEP TRYING LEARNING UNTIL I CAN.

I CAN'T DO....

WAYS I CAN GET THERE....

BECAUSE I....

DRAW A PICTURE TO SHOW HOW YOU USE YOUR BEAUTIFUL BRAIN TO SOLVE A PROBLEM.

GROWTH MINDSET THE POWER OF YET ACTIVITY

DATE:

S   M   T   W   TH   F   S   ___/___/___

I CAN DO MANY THING.

....

1) I CAN:

....

....

....

2) I CAN:

....

....

....

3) I CAN:

....

....

....

SOME TING THAT I CANT'T DO YET, BUT I WILL KEEP TRYING LEARNING UNTIL I CAN.

I CAN'T DO....

....

....

....

WAYS I CAN GET THERE....

....

....

....

BECAUSE I....

....

....

....

DRAW A PICTURE TO SHOW HOW YOU USE YOUR BEAUTIFUL BRAIN TO SOLVE A PROBLEM.

GROWTH MINDSET THE POWER OF YET ACTIVITY

DATE:

S   M   T   W   TH   F   S   __/__/__

I CAN DO MANY THING.

1) I CAN:

2) I CAN:

3) I CAN:

SOME TING THAT I CANT'T DO YET, BUT I WILL KEEP TRYING LEARNING UNTIL I CAN.

I CAN'T DO....

WAYS I CAN GET THERE....

BECAUSE I....

DRAW A PICTURE TO SHOW HOW YOU USE YOUR BEAUTIFUL BRAIN TO SOLVE A PROBLEM.

GROWTH MINDSET THE POWER OF YET ACTIVITY

DATE:

S   M   T   W   TH   F   S   __ / __ / __

I CAN DO MANY THING.

....

1) I CAN:

....

....

....

2) I CAN:

....

....

....

3) I CAN:

....

....

SOME TING THAT I CANT'T DO YET, BUT I WILL KEEP TRYING LEARNING UNTIL I CAN.

I CAN'T DO....

....

....

....

WAYS I CAN GET THERE....

....

....

....

BECAUSE I....

....

....

....

DRAW A PICTURE TO SHOW HOW YOU USE YOUR BEAUTIFUL BRAIN TO SOLVE A PROBLEM.

GROWTH MINDSET THE POWER OF YET ACTIVITY

DATE:

S   M   T   W   TH   F   S   __/__/__

I CAN DO MANY THING.

....

1) I CAN:

....

....

2) I CAN:

....

....

3) I CAN:

....

....

SOME TING THAT I CANT'T DO YET, BUT I WILL KEEP TRYING LEARNING UNTIL I CAN.

I CAN'T DO....

....

....

....

WAYS I CAN GET THERE....

....

....

....

BECAUSE I....

....

....

....

DRAW A PICTURE TO SHOW HOW YOU USE YOUR BEAUTIFUL BRAIN TO SOLVE A PROBLEM.

GROWTH MINDSET THE POWER OF YET ACTIVITY

DATE:

S   M   T   W   TH   F   S   ___/___/___

I CAN DO MANY THING.

1) I CAN:

2) I CAN:

3) I CAN:

SOME TING THAT I CANT'T DO YET, BUT I WILL
KEEP TRYING LEARNING UNTIL I CAN.

I CAN'T DO....

....

....

....

WAYS I CAN GET THERE....

....

....

....

BECAUSE I....

....

....

....

DRAW A PICTURE TO SHOW HOW YOU USE YOUR BEAUTIFUL BRAIN TO SOLVE A PROBLEM.

GROWTH MINDSET THE POWER OF YET ACTIVITY

DATE:

S   M   T   W   TH   F   S   __/__/__

I CAN DO MANY THING.

1) I CAN:

2) I CAN:

3) I CAN:

SOME TING THAT I CANT'T DO YET, BUT I WILL KEEP TRYING LEARNING UNTIL I CAN.

I CAN'T DO....

WAYS I CAN GET THERE....

BECAUSE I....

DRAW A PICTURE TO SHOW HOW YOU USE YOUR BEAUTIFUL BRAIN TO SOLVE A PROBLEM.

GROWTH MINDSET THE POWER OF YET ACTIVITY

DATE:

S   M   T   W   TH   F   S   __/__/__

I CAN DO MANY THING.

1) I CAN:

2) I CAN:

3) I CAN:

SOME TING THAT I CANT'T DO YET, BUT I WILL KEEP TRYING LEARNING UNTIL I CAN.

I CAN'T DO....

WAYS I CAN GET THERE....

BECAUSE I....

DRAW A PICTURE TO SHOW HOW YOU USE YOUR BEAUTIFUL BRAIN TO SOLVE A PROBLEM.

GROWTH MINDSET THE POWER OF YET ACTIVITY

DATE:

S   M   T   W   TH   F   S   __/__/__

I CAN DO MANY THING.

1) I CAN:

2) I CAN:

3) I CAN:

SOME TING THAT I CANT'T DO YET, BUT I WILL KEEP TRYING LEARNING UNTIL I CAN.

I CAN'T DO....

WAYS I CAN GET THERE....

BECAUSE I....

I FEEL:     

DRAW A PICTURE TO SHOW HOW YOU USE YOUR BEAUTIFUL BRAIN TO SOLVE A PROBLEM.

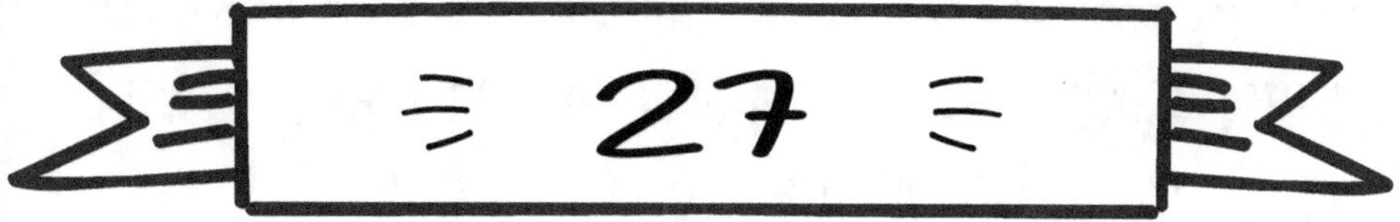

GROWTH MINDSET THE POWER OF YET ACTIVITY

DATE:

S   M   T   W   TH   F   S   __/__/__

I CAN DO MANY THING.

....

1) I CAN:
....

....

....

2) I CAN:
....

....

....

3) I CAN:
....

....

SOME TING THAT I CANT'T DO YET, BUT I WILL KEEP TRYING LEARNING UNTIL I CAN.

I CAN'T DO....

....

....

....

WAYS I CAN GET THERE....

....

....

....

BECAUSE I....

....

....

....

DRAW A PICTURE TO SHOW HOW YOU USE YOUR BEAUTIFUL BRAIN TO SOLVE A PROBLEM.

GROWTH MINDSET THE POWER OF YET ACTIVITY

DATE:

S   M   T   W   TH   F   S   __/__/__

I CAN DO MANY THING.

1) I CAN:

2) I CAN:

3) I CAN:

SOME TING THAT I CANT'T DO YET, BUT I WILL KEEP TRYING LEARNING UNTIL I CAN.

I CAN'T DO....

....

....

....

WAYS I CAN GET THERE....

....

....

....

BECAUSE I....

....

....

....

DRAW A PICTURE TO SHOW HOW YOU USE YOUR BEAUTIFUL BRAIN TO SOLVE A PROBLEM.

GROWTH MINDSET THE POWER OF YET ACTIVITY

DATE:

S   M   T   W   TH   F   S   ___/___/___

I CAN DO MANY THING.

1) I CAN:

2) I CAN:

3) I CAN:

SOME TING THAT I CANT'T DO YET, BUT I WILL KEEP TRYING LEARNING UNTIL I CAN.

I CAN'T DO....

WAYS I CAN GET THERE....

BECAUSE I....

DRAW A PICTURE TO SHOW HOW YOU USE YOUR
BEAUTIFUL BRAIN TO SOLVE A PROBLEM.

GROWTH MINDSET THE POWER OF YET ACTIVITY

DATE:

S   M   T   W   TH   F   S   ___/___/___

I CAN DO MANY THING.

1) I CAN:

2) I CAN:

3) I CAN:

SOME TING THAT I CANT'T DO YET, BUT I WILL KEEP TRYING LEARNING UNTIL I CAN.

I CAN'T DO....

WAYS I CAN GET THERE....

BECAUSE I....

DRAW A PICTURE TO SHOW HOW YOU USE YOUR BEAUTIFUL BRAIN TO SOLVE A PROBLEM.

100 FUN IDEAS

Go fishing
Go rock hunting
Go on a nature walk
Blow bubbles
Stargaze
Build a sandcastle
Fly a kite
Have a picnic
Finger Paint
Make paper bag puppets
Make Tie-Dye Shirts
Make paper boats
Make Story Stones
Make A Bird Feeder
Write a Story and Illustrate It
Make Friendship Bracelets
Catch Fireflies
Play At The Park with Friends
Watch Fireworks
Dance In The Rain
Play Frisbee
Watch The Sunset At the Beach
Watch A Thunderstorm
Collect Seashells
Bonfire and S'mores
Watch The Sunrise At the Beach
Make Wishes on Dandelions
Climb A Tree
Plant Flowers
Build A Sand Castle
Jump in Puddles
Plant Vegetables
Go Cloud Watching
Jump on A Trampoline
Go Kayaking
Bury A Time Capsule
Random Acts of Kindness
Donate To An Animal Shelter
Write a Soldier a Letter
Visit A Nursing Home
Make Cookies For A Neighbor
Host A Scavenger Hunt
PJ Movie Day
Start a Blessings Jar
Make A Blanket Fort
Start A Summer Journal
Family Game Night
Play Bingo
Play Capture the Flag
Have A Slumber Party

Drive-in Movie Theatre
Visit an aquarium
Go to a children's museum
Go to a water park
Go To the Library
Visit national monuments
Visit A Farmer's Market
Visit Mom or Dad at Work
Go Camping
Go on a Nature Walk
Visit A Water Park
Visit A Zoo
Attend A Free Kids Workshop
Ride Your Bike on a Trail
Go Mini Golfing
Go Bowling
Go Rock Hunting
Go To Chuck E Cheese
Ride a Ferris Wheel
Marco Polo
Run Through Sprinklers
Water Balloon Fight
Make Sponge Water Bombs
Go Swimming
Wash the Family Car
Make and Sail Paper Boats
Play on a Slip 'n Slide
Have a Water Fight
Make Homemade Ice Cream
Eat Watermelon
Roast Marshmallows
Eat A Snowcone
Make Rootbeer Floats
Eat Breakfast For Dinner
Eat Popsicles
Help Cook Dinner
Make Fresh Lemonade
Make Homemade Pizza
Drink A Slurpee
Buy From the Ice Cream Truck
Read At Least 10 Books
Do A Science Project
Learn Origami
Attend a Free Kids Art Class
Play Hide And Seek
Play Dodgeball
Play Flashlight Tag
Play Messy Twister
Play Tag with Friends
Have a Pillow Fight

IF YOU NEVER TRY
YOU WILL NEVER KNOW

9 798645 211516